C000162219

Purple Ronnie's
Star Signs

Libra
23rd September - 22nd October

☆

First published 1994 by Statics (London) Ltd

This edition published 2002 by Boxtree
an imprint of Pan Macmillan Ltd
Pan Macmillan, 20 New Wharf Road, London N1 9RR
Basingstoke and Oxford
Associated companies throughout the world
www.panmacmillan.com

ISBN 0 7522 2049 7

A CIP catalogue record for this book is available from
the British Library

Text by Giles Andreae
Illustrations by Janet Cronin
Printed and bound in Hong Kong

☆ Introduction ☆

Star Signs are a brilliant way of finding out about someone's character. You can use them to discover anything you like including what everyone's secretest rude fantasies are.

But reading what's written in the stars can only be done by incredibly brainy people like me. After gazing for ages through my gigantic telescope and doing loads of complicated sums and

charts and stuff I have been able to
work out exactly what everyone in the
world is really like.

This book lets you know about all my
amazing discoveries. It tells you what you
look like, who your friends are, how your
love life is, what you're like at Doing It
and who you should be Doing It with.
Everything I've written in this book is
completely true. Honest.

Love from

Purple Ronnie
xox

Contents

They like to share their feelings
They simply can't pretend
They make you feel that you're their only
Special bestest friend

☆ Libra Looks ☆

As soon as you look at a Libran you think they're lovely which is why Librans spend so much time looking at themselves

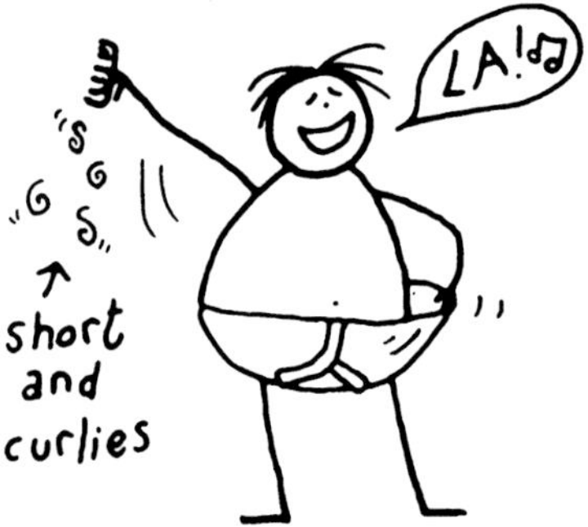
LA!
short and curlies

Libra Men

Libra Men have voices that make girls go all swoony. They like to comb the hair on their dangly bits and they always wear clean pants

Libra Women

Libra Women have curvy bodies, sexy faces and the scrumptiousest smiles in the world

☆Libra Character☆

Librans want everything to be beautiful and lovely. They adore grown-up music, gorgeous outfits, pretty pictures and twirly dancing

Librans are totally useless

☆ Libra and Friends ☆

Librans hate being on their own so they always go everywhere with lots of friends

ooh I don't like his sandals... ... nice bum though... aah this is my favourite bit... doesn't he blow up the baddies?...
sigh

Warning:-

Librans love nattering and they are never stuck for things to say

FASHION DESIGNERS

because:-

1. They love arty type stuff and like to make everything match

2. They are often moody and stroppy and easy to upset

3. They prefer to be neat and clean and tidy to sweaty and dirty and messy

☆ Libra and Love ☆

Librans love the idea of being in love...

...and they long to be swept off their feet

Love for a Libran is more about friendly cuddles than mad snogging and passionate sex

Librans like to look good
so they usually fall in love...

...with
very
beautiful
People...

...or
very
ugly
people

☆ Libra and Sex ☆

Librans love flirting
and are brilliant at
making you want to
Do It with them

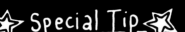 Special Tip

Some Librans prefer
reading about sex to
actually Doing It

But when a Libran wants to Do It with you they like to make sure it's the best sex you've ever had

The End